Steve King
. 9.1

JOINING THE CHURCH

Also available in the "How To Series"

Praying the Lord's Prayer	Terry Virgo
Effective Evangelism	Ben Davies
Growing Up As A Christian	Roger Day
Handling Your Money	John Houghton
Learning To Worship	Phil Rogers
Leading A Housegroup	Richard Haydon-Knowell
Presenting Jesus In The Open Air	Mike Sprenger with Mary Austin

For further information on the "How To Series" and New Frontiers International, please write to New Frontiers International, 21-23 Clarendon Villas, Hove, Brighton, East Sussex, BN3 3RE.

SERIES EDITOR
TERRY VIRGO

How to...
STUDY SERIES

JOINING THE CHURCH

RICHARD HAYDON-KNOWELL

NEWFRONTIERS

WORD PUBLISHING

Word (UK) Ltd
Milton Keynes, England

WORD AUSTRALIA
Heathmont, Victoria, Australia
STRUIK CHRISTIAN BOOKS (PTY) LTD
Salt River, South Africa
ALBY COMMERCIAL ENTERPRISES PTE LTD
Balmoral Road, Singapore
CONCORDE DISTRIBUTORS LTD
Havelock North, New Zealand
CROSS (HK) CO
Hong Kong

JOINING THE CHURCH

First published by Coastlands.
Revised edition 1988 Word (UK) Ltd/New Frontiers.

ISBN 0-85009-182-9 (Australia 1-86258-051-6)

Printed and bound in Great Britain by Cox & Wyman Ltd., Reading.

INTRODUCTION

The 'How to' series has been published with a definite purpose in view. It provides a set of workbooks suitable either for housegroups or individuals who want to study a particular Bible theme in a practical way. The goal is not simply to look up verses and fill in blank spaces on the page, but to fill in gaps in our lives and so increase our fruitfulness and our knowledge of God.

Peter wrote his letters to 'stimulate wholesome thinking' (2 Peter 3:1). He required his readers to think as well as read! We hope the training manual approach of this book will have the same effect. *Stop, think, apply* and *act* are key words.

If you are using the book on your own, we suggest you work through the chapters systematically, Bible at your side and pen in hand. If you are doing it as a group activity, it is probably best to do all the initial reading and task work before the group sessions - this gives more time for discussion on key issues which may be raised.

All quotations from the Bible are from the New International Version, which the reader is expected to use in filling in the study material.

Terry Virgo
Series Editor

NEW FRONTIERS INTERNATIONAL is a team ministry led by Terry Virgo and involved in planting and equipping churches according to New Testament principles with a view to reaching this generation with the gospel of the Kingdom. They are also responsible for a wide range of conferences, training programmes and the production of printed and audio teaching materials.

Contents

WHAT THE COURSE IS ALL ABOUT

The Scriptures teach that it is God's will for all Christians to belong to a local church where they can be cared for, loved and taught, so being helped to grow in spiritual maturity and become good soldiers of Jesus Christ.

The course is designed to do two things:-

First, to teach from the Scriptures what God's basic requirements are for belonging to His church. This first part of the course is concerned with judgment to come, repentance, faith, baptism in water and baptism in the Holy Spirit.

Second, to teach what it means to become part of a local church. We shall look at matters like leadership, housegroups, commitment, serving each other, financial support and fellowship together.

Those who are newly converted will find it very helpful to do both Part One and Part Two which will last seven weeks. Mature Christians who wish to join a church may, if they wish and at the discretion of their leadership, just do the second part of this course.

We trust that you will find the course really helpful and upbuilding, and that by the time it is completed you and your leaders will have come to know God's will about your joining the church.

Part One

BECOMING A CHRISTIAN

One of the most important parts of this course is the reading of the Scriptures in advance of the lesson.

During the week prior to each lesson you will need to read the various passages from the Bible as indicated on the next page, except for Lesson 1 where the readings are included in the lesson. There is a reading for each day of the week. Please read these in a modern version of the Bible such as the New International Version or the New American Standard Bible. God's Word is able to make you wise for salvation through faith in Christ Jesus (2 Timothy 3:15).

N.B. If you are not sure how to find the readings, for instance 2 Timothy 3:15, look up the name of Timothy the author in the index at the front of your Bible. The number 2 before his name shows that this is his second book. The number 3 indicates that the reference is in the third chapter, usually printed in large black type. The number 15 is the number of the verse to look for. If you run your eye down the page you will see the verse numbers in very small type.

The lesson material should be read through, verses looked up and filled in, and questions answered, prior to each lesson. This 'home study' is important and forms a vital part of the course. We want you to learn to examine the Scriptures for yourself and to become familiar with them.

Please make sure you do this week by week. It is helpful too if the course leader looks through these with you during the lesson and, if possible, goes through the whole book with you on completion of the course. Don't be afraid to ask questions if there are things you don't understand. There is a blank page at the end of the book for personal notes or for recording questions which you may wish to ask your course leader.

Scriptures to read prior to the lessons		
Lesson 2	**Lesson 3**	**Lesson 4**
Day 1 Matt. 7:24-29	Matthew 28:16-20	Luke 24:13-53
Day 2 Acts 2:22-41	Matthew 3:1-17	Acts 1:1-11
Day 3 Acts 16:16-40	Acts 8:26-40	1 Cor. 14:1-28
Day 4 Eph. 2:1-10	Acts 9:1-19, 22:16	1 Cor. 12:1-31
Day 5 Gen. 2:15 - 3:24	Romans 6:1-14	1 Cor. 2:1-16
Day 6 Isaiah 53:1-12	2 Timothy 1:1-14	Galatians 5:13-26
Day 7 Mark 15:1-47	Acts 19:1-7	Luke 11:1-13

Lesson 1
JUDGMENT TO COME

Does it seem strange to you to begin a course of basic Bible teaching with a lesson on that judgment by God which is to come? If so, remember that the world we live in is God's world and it therefore makes sense for us to learn something about God Himself.

GOD IS OUR JUDGE

Today many say 'God is love', but we must understand that God is also our judge. It is because He will judge all men according to their deeds that we need to know a salvation that will deliver us from eternal judgment and condemnation.

As creator He has authority to judge

God has made us and has authority to make laws for us - laws which are right and which are made for our good. They are not unreasonable or thoughtless but loving and wise. God is just and will reward or punish us according to whether we keep His laws or not.

As the all-knowing God He is able to judge

Human judgment is, even at its best, hindered by the inability to know all the facts, and especially by the inability to know what goes on in a person's heart and secret, inner thoughts. Not so with God. God knows all things. He knows our actions and our thoughts. We can fool others but we cannot fool God.

Turn to 1 Samuel 16:7 and write down what it says about the difference between man's judging and God's judging.

Man looks at ....

The Lord looks at ....

GOD HAS ACTED IN JUDGMENT IN HUMAN HISTORY

It is a mistake to think that judgment is just a thing of the future. It is not! God has acted in judgment throughout the history of mankind as can be seen from the following examples:

Adam and Eve were expelled from the garden of Eden - Genesis 3

Noah's generation was judged by the flood - Genesis 6-8

Sodom and Gomorrah were overthrown - Genesis 18,19

Israel's cruel Egyptian slave masters were destroyed after the warnings of the ten plagues - Exodus 7:12

God judged Israel for the nation's frequent unfaithfulness - the book of Judges

God judged the Jews for rejecting Christ - Matthew 21: 43-44

Ananias and Sapphira were judged for lying to God -Acts 5

Elymas was struck with blindness for his opposition to the gospel - Acts 13

The Corinthian Christians suffered for their misuse of the Lord's Supper - 1 Corinthians 11:29-32

THERE IS A JUDGMENT TO COME

The judgment of men and women while they are alive, which we saw in the previous section, is not the only judgment spoken about in the Bible. It is there as a warning, as a solemn pointer to a more complete and certain day of universal judgment. The New Testament frequently refers to this day:

See Acts 17-31 For he has set ....

....

According to Paul's gospel (Romans 2:61), God will ....

....

What three phrases are used to summarise Paul's preaching to Felix in Acts 24:25?

....

....

....

We must all appear

Please fill in the gaps:

2 Corinthians 5:10 For we must .... appear before the judgment seat of Christ, that .... may receive ....

....

Matthew 16:27 For the Son of Man is going to come in his Father's glory with his angels, and then he will ....

....

Revelation 22:12 Behold, I am coming soon! My reward is with me, and I will give..

....

How many will avoid this?..

On what will the judgment be based? ....

We shall give an account

We are all responsible creatures and so we shall not only be punished or rewarded but also required to give an account of ourselves to God. In this life we are all too well aware of our natural tendency to judge others and point out their faults and failings, whilst excusing our own. The New Testament says something very strong about this: Read Romans 14:10-12.

What sort of detail does Matthew 12:36 tell us about this account that we must give?...

What phrases in the following verses show how thorough God's judgment of our lives will be?

Romans 2:16 ....

Luke 12:2-3 ....

....

....

Revelation 2:23 ....

....

1 Corinthians 4:5 ....

....

The character of God demands that all wrongs will one day be righted: when 'the day of God's wrath and righteous judgment' arrives reward or punishment will be exact. Justice will be done. Nothing unfair will remain to haunt us. Just as God is perfect in every other act, He will be perfect in judgment.

If God took no notice of our sin, would that be a good thing or a bad thing?

....

Final judgment will be according to our response to the knowledge of God

Judgment has not only to do with our deeds but also with our response to the revelation that God has made of Himself - in creation; in our consciences; in the Scriptures and through His Son. Romans 1:18-23 teaches that even if people have not specifically heard the gospel of Christ there is sufficient of God's power and glory present in creation to make the rejection of God 'without excuse'. Please also look at Romans 2:12 and Luke 12:47-49. It is not for us to debate these things from our feeble ability to judge, but rather to face up to our responsibilities as those who comparatively speaking 'know much'. We need to turn wholeheartedly to Jesus who was sent into the world:

not to ....

but to .... (John 3:17)

Our next study will show God's way of salvation. This salvation does not of course mean that we will not have to give an account of our lives to God, but it does make **all the difference** to our ultimate destiny and our present enjoyment and experience of forgiveness and acceptance with God.

Those who have become Christians, having been justified (that is, declared righteous in God's sight because of what Christ has done for them) will still have their lives assessed by God - but it will be with an entirely different outcome. The Christian who is slack or disobedient will certainly lose his reward though he himself will be saved. Look up 1 Corinthians 3:12-15 and note carefully what is to be tested and the outcome of that testing. The unbeliever, however, being without salvation, will be altogether lost for ever in that Day. (Revelation 20:11-15).

What is your reaction to this lesson?

Perhaps you are a new Christian and it only confirms your worst fears that Christianity is full of gloom and doom. That's an understandable reaction but we cannot bury our heads in the sands - judgment is real! However, in Christ we have a glorious salvation which delivers us totally from the wrath to come. Right now: lift up your heart to God in praise, thanksgiving and love for Jesus who 'bore our sins in His body on the tree, so that we might die to sin and live for righteousness'.

One final thing. Has this lesson helped you to understand not only the offensiveness of sin and the need for judgment but also the tremendous love of God in sending His Son to save sinful people? Well, we have been entrusted with this good news. During this coming week ask God for an opportunity to share God's 'love message' with a friend or relative.

Our second lesson will be about repentance and faith.

Lesson 2
REPENTANCE AND FAITH IN THE LORD JESUS

Scriptures to read before this lesson	
Day 1	Mathew 7:24-29
Day 2	Acts 2:22-41
Day 3	Acts 16:16-40
Day 4	Ephesians 2:1-10
Day 5	Genesis 2:15 - 3:24
Day 6	Isaiah 53:1-12
Day 7	Mark 15:1-47

BUILDING ON A FIRM FOUNDATION

At the end of a long series of teaching Jesus told a story about two men who each built a house. (See Day 1 of your reading plan).

The point of the story is plain - if you only hear, and fail to put into practice what you have heard, your house (or rather your life, for that is what the story is about) will have no foundation and will collapse. **Hearing** and **doing** are both vital.

You do not become a Christian by just hearing about God's way of salvation. There has to be a 'doing' also.

HEARING AND DOING

The Apostle Peter preached about the death and resurrection of the Lord Jesus Christ. Those who heard this preaching were deeply convictd about their sin and unbelief and their rejection of God's Son. They cried out, 'What shall we do?' (Acts 2 verse 37).

Similarly, in the passage in Acts 16 that you read on Day 3, the jailer, having heard the apostles rejoicing in the midst of their sufferings, and having seen the power of God at work, cried out, 'What must I do to be saved?' (verse 30).

Now, write down what both Peter and Paul told them to do.

Acts 2:38 ....

....

....

Acts 2:40 ....

Acts 16:31 ....

....

BEING SAVED

Both Peter and Paul speak about 'being saved'. This is another way of saying 'becoming a Christian' - actually it is a more accurate way of saying it; for it tells us that we are lost and need to be found; captured and need to be delivered; dead and need to be brought to life.

In fact the Bible uses many descriptions to show us how 'lost' or 'dead' we really are.

Can you see four such descriptions in the passage you read from Ephesians 2 verses 1-32? Write them down.

Verse 1 **You were** ....

Verse 2 **You followed** ....

....

....

Verse 3 **All of us** ....

....

....

Verse 3 **We were** ....

This is a devastating, but nevertheless true, description of every single person on the earth. Because by nature we are sinful, dead to God, deceived and led on by Satan (the ruler of the kingdom of the air), we follow the cravings and strong desires of our sinful nature. We are spiritually in darkness and, as the Bible puts it, in the 'Kingdom of darkness' itself.

You may be thinking, 'How did all this come about? How is it that mankind (and I in particular) came to be like this?' To answer that question we shall need to go back to the beginning.

When God created our foreparents, Adam and Eve, He created them as beautiful, good and intelligent people. He made them in His own image or likeness. But they were on trial. You will have read what happened in your reading from Genesis chapter 3. When they sinned, through disobedience and wanting to be 'independent of God', not only did they fall and become slaves of sin and Satan, but the entire human race, yet unborn, fell with them. Each of us has personally endorsed Adam's choice by similarly choosing to live independently of God and wanting to do our own thing. It isn't that every single act is sinful, for by God's grace there are many fine, splendid and humanitarian things which men and women do; rather the whole direction of our lives is self-centred and not God-centred.

It is from all that we need to be saved. But how?

GOD'S RESCUE OPERATION

The Bible makes it clear that we cannot save ourselves by ourselves. **God** has done something. Salvation is from God. Let us look at some Scriptures and see how they teach that salvation is something God has initiated and provided.

Look at Galatians 1 verses 3-5	NOTE CAREFULLY HOW GOD
Look at John 3 verse 16	TAKES THE INITIATIVE

....

....

....

God's plan was to send His own Son, the Lord Jesus Christ, to be born of the virgin Mary, in order that He might truly be man. The

Bible speaks of Him as the 'second man' (1 Corinthians 15 verse 47). Jesus, unlike Adam the 'first man', did not sin. He lived a life of absolute righteousness. He was tempted in every way just as Adam was and we are, but He did not sin: His was a perfect life.

Then why did He die? Can you remember what Isaiah wrote in Chapter 53?

Peter sums it up for us in just a few words. Look them up and write out what it says (1 Peter 3 verse 18).

....

.... to bring you to God.

His death was 'to bring you to God'. He died as your substitute, and mine. He took our guilt, our sin, and made Himself responsible for what we had done. God then punished His own dear Son for sins we had committed, so that sin might be properly dealt with, and thus made forgiveness and acceptance possible for us. God can't just let sinners off, any more than a human judge can!

Have you ever wondered why Jesus cried out on the cross, 'My God, my God, why have you forsaken me?' Are you beginning to understand now?

Write down why you think He said this, in your own words.

....

....

....

You may also wonder why Jesus rose again. God raised Him because He had fully paid our debt by His sufferings on the cross, and by His entering into death itself for us. And, of course, because He completely triumphed over Satan. (We will come back to this in a later lesson.)

But just now; do you remember that earlier in this lesson we saw that **we** had to both hear and do something? We have seen what **God** did. What do we have to do? Peter and Paul put it like this: 'Repent'; 'Believe in the Lord Jesus Christ'.

REPENTANCE AND FAITH

Repentance is the first foundation stone of the Christian life. What do you think repentance is? Tick which you think is most correct.

1. Saying sorry ☐
2. Promising not to sin again ☐
3. Trying to do better in the future ☐
4. Turning from sin and self-rule to God ☐

Repentance is more than just being sorry - it is a total about-turn, a change of our whole attitude towards sin and God. Real repentance is not a once-and-for-all-time experience; it is the beginning of a way of life which involves turning from everything which is not pleasing to God.

Look at the following Scriptures and write down the actions which demonstrate true repentance.

2 Kings 23 verses 24, 25 ....

....

Luke 3 verses 7-14 ....

....

(These were all very practical, down-to-earth, life changing things weren't they?)

Have **you** repented of your sin and ungodliness? If so, is there any clear 'fruit' or evidence of repentance in your life to show that you have turned to the Lord with all your heart?

Write it down ....

....

....

Coupled with turning from sin and ungodliness is believing in the Lord Jesus. The word **'believe'** means 'trust in', 'put faith in', 'rely upon'. It is a very active word. When Adam and Even sinned they began putting faith in themselves, relying upon their own resources, good deeds and so on. All men and women are like them, trusting to their own efforts.

When God begins to open our eyes, we begin to see how frail and hopeless our own efforts are to save us from sin, Satan's power and God's righteous judgment. But as we have seen God has provided the Saviour who really can save us. To believe in Him means to trust in Him, put your faith in Him, and rely upon Him to save you.

Have you done this? YES/NO

If you have, will you write below in your own words, very briefly, **when you put your faith in Him** and **how you know** He has saved you.

....

....

....

....

....

(If you find this impossible to express in writing, then do share it with your course leader by word of mouth.)

If the answer to the question was 'NO', then you will probably want to talk to him in any case about this.

THE BLESSINGS OF SALVATION

When we believe in Christ we are **justified** (Romans 5:1). So thoroughly and effectively has Christ dealt with our sin by His death on the cross that all the just claims of the holy law of God have been met in full. The sentence having been paid, we are justified before God. That is, there are no outstanding claims against us. We stand eternally acquitted before God - we are seen as though we had never sinned! Nothing can alter our standing before God in this respect for it has been secured for us by the death and resurrection of the Lord Jesus Christ.

Another blessing which flows from this is our **acceptance** before God. In God's marvellous plan of salvation Christ took upon Himself all our sins and wrongdoing. He was 'made sin for us' (2 Corinthians 5:21). But that is only half of the amazing plan. He was made sin for us that 'in Him we might become the righteousness of God'. That means that when we are united by faith to Jesus all the virtue of His holy life, all the merits of His complete obedience to God, are put to our account. They are made over to us so that we can now appear before God through Christ with all the merits He has won for us.

What do you think about about that? ....

....

We are also now **adopted** into God's family as sons - look up Ephesians 1:4-5. What does sonship mean? Look up and write down the key words describing the privileges and responsibilities of sonship from the following references:

Galatians 4:6-7 ....

Matthew 6:26-32 ....

Romans 8:15-17 ....

Before we finish this lesson there is one more very important thing.

You will remember that earlier in this lesson we learnt that Satan has a kingdom - he has under him many evil spirit-beings who seek to carry out his purposes of deceiving men and women, secretly encouraging them to live ungodly and sinful lives and blinding them to the truth. These spirits are actively at work behind all false religions like Hinduism, Buddhism and so on, as well as perversions and distortions of true Christianity like Christian Science, Mormonism, the Jehovah Witness teaching and others. They are also deeply involved in, and promote, occult practices like satanism, spiritism, horoscopes, ouija boards, clairvoyance, and even transcendental meditation and drug taking. Not only that but they actively look out for and seek to have a harmful effect on people who may have been deeply hurt emotionally, (perhaps in childhood) or who have been drawn into sexual immorality or deviation.

Sometimes people's involvement in these things has been as a 'victim' rather than as someone who knowingly wanted to get involved. Nevertheless, if you are such a person you may have been affected in the depth of your personality and may require help by prayer and counsel from the leaders of the church. If you have been in any of the above or something similar, please mention it to the course leader or indicate it with a tick. ☐

The next lesson is about this new life which we enter through repentance and faith, and we shall learn why BAPTISM is so important.

Lesson 3
BAPTISM IN WATER

Scriptures to read before this lesson	
Day 1	Matthew 28:16-20
Day 2	Matthew 3:1-17
Day 3	Acts 8:26-40
Day 4	Acts 9:1-19, 22:16
Day 5	Romans 6: 1-14
Day 6	2 Timothy 1:1-14
Day 7	Acts 19:1-7

ANOTHER PART OF THE FOUNDATION

In Lesson 2 we saw that repentance and faith are foundational to salvation. From your reading of the Scriptures you will have discovered that very closely linked to repentance and faith is baptism. Baptism is not simply a tradition of 'Baptist' churches - it has its origin in the life and teaching of the Lord Jesus and the practice of the church from the very beginning.

In simple terms baptism is a 'putting of the new convert under water and raising him again in the name of the Lord'. But because there is so much confusion and misunderstanding about it, and because it is so important, we will need to look carefully at the Scriptures. Let's begin by asking 'Why?', 'Who?', 'How?' and 'What?'

WHY SHOULD WE BE BAPTISED?

It is the command of the Lord Jesus Christ. That should really settle the matter for every Christian - Look up Matthew 28 verses 16-

20. Write down the three things that Jesus told His disciples to do (two are found in verse 19 and the third is in verse 20).

1. ....

2. ....

....

3. ....

....

In that three-fold command you have a very clear statement of one of the church's main functions. This is exactly what the early church began to do, as you will remember from your readings in Acts. It is also what we are doing right now: helping you to become a desciple (that is someone who is committed to the Lord Jesus and desires to follow Him with all his heart); preparing you to be baptised; and teaching you to obey all His commands.

A second reason why we are to be baptised is because **the Lord Jesus gave us an example to follow.** See Matthew 3 verses 13-17. John obviously felt that it wasn't 'right' for Jesus to be baptised. Jesus had committed no sin; Jesus wasn't unrighteous like those that John had been baptising in the river Jordan. Note Jesus's answer. 'Let it be so now; it is proper for us to do this to fulfil all righteousness' (verse 15). Jesus came to 'fulfil and do all righteousness'. Though He had no sin of His own, He had come to take the sinner's place and to bring God's righteousness to sinners. If it was 'proper' for **Him**, is it not for **us** who have received that righteousness?

Before we leave Jesus' baptism, look down at verses 16 and 17. What two things happened immediately after He was baptised?

1. ....

2. ....

....

Do you think this should follow your baptism?

WHO SHOULD BE BAPTISED?

The New Testament makes it clear that baptism is **only** for those who have repented of sin and believed in the Lord Jesus Christ.

Jesus taught this - Matthew 28:19, Mark 16:16

The church did this - Acts 2:41, 8:12, 8:36-38, 9:17-18, 10:47-48, 16:14-15, 16:31-34, 18:8 and 19:4-5

(There probably won't be time to look up **all** the above references but turn to at least one or two).

A common question is, 'What if a person was baptised or christened as a baby? Should he be baptised now that he is a believer?' The answer is 'YES'. Christening (or infant baptism) is **not** taught in the Bible. Baptism is for believers **only**. Even in a case like that of the Philippian jailer in the New Testament, where children may have been included in the household, their baptism was right. **See why for yourself** in Acts 16 verses 32-34:

They spoke the word of the Lord to ....

in his house . . . . Immediately he and ....were

baptised baptised . . . . And the .... was filled with

joy, because ....in God.

HOW SHOULD WE BE BAPTISED?

The word 'baptism' in Greek, the original language of the New Testament, means to 'dip', 'immerse', 'submerge or plunge' into a liquid. It is used to describe the dyeing of cloth, sinking of ships, and so on. To be baptised means to be immersed in water. The New Testament baptism was by immersion.

Look at two examples:

JESUS (Mark 1:10) 'As Jesus was coming **up out of the water** ...'

THE ETHOPIAN CONVERT (Acts 8:39) 'Both Philip and the eunuch **went down into the water** and Philip baptised him. When they came **up out of the water** ...'

Baptism by immersion is important for it is meant to help us enter into some very vital life-changing experiences. Look carefully at

Romans 6 verses 1-4 and write down the three words which describe the experience of the Lord Jesus which we share through baptism.

d ...., b................................ and r ....

I think you will readily agree that baptism by immersion, with its plunging into the water, putting under and lifting up out of the water, very clearly represents Jesus' immersion into death, burial and resurrection.

WHAT IS THE MEANING AND PURPOSE OF BAPTISM?

The Bible says a lot about baptism and it will not be possible to include everything in this short course. But here are some of the main things baptism does for us:

1. It is a uniting with Jesus in His death, burial and resurrection.

Keep your Bible open at Romans 6 verses 1-14. Paul tells us that it is unnatural for Christians to go on sinning.

Do dead people sin? YES/NO

The point he is making is this: When Jesus suffered on the cross He was totally under the power of sin. His death was a proof of it. But by dying and being buried, He was freed from the power of sin. It is like a person in prison. All the time he is there he is under the power of the jailer. When he is discharged the jailer has lost his power and authority over him. He is free!

By our baptism we share in this death-burial-resurrection experience of the Lord Jesus. We are baptised 'in His name' into His death, burial and resurrection in the water. The devil will (like the jailer, perhaps) try and kid us that we are still under the power of sin. We need to reply, 'NO! By being united to Jesus in baptism I died to sin and am now alive to God'. That is the wonderful truth of your baptism.

When you are baptised will you go into the water believing this? ....

We are constantly to think of ourselves like that. Which verse in the passage in Romans 6 tells us to do that?

Verse 5...................... Verse 8 .... Verse 11 ....

(Tick correct verse.)

Does this mean that once a Christian is baptised he will never sin again? Not exactly, it means that we need not sin, or, to put it positively, we could live holy and righteous lives just like Jesus, who fully trusted and obeyed His Father. But the truth is we often forget to trust Him, or we yield to Satan's temptations or sin's attractiveness, or selfishly please ourselves. That doesn't mean we cease to be Christians or need to be re-baptised. We can never lose our salvation! And because sin's power has been really broken these lapses (for which we should ask and receive God's forgiveness - see 1 John 1:7-10) should become less and less.

2. Baptism is also a way of expressing our total commitment to God.

Have you noticed how the words 'in the name' or 'into the name' of Jesus or of Father, Son and Holy Spirit are used in connection with baptism? We are familiar with that expression in the world of commerce. When you sell a car or house, it is transferred into the name of the new owner on payment of the purchase price. Thereafter the new owner has absolute rights over it! It is so in baptism. The Lord Jesus by His death on the cross purchases us - in our baptism we are voluntarily giving ourselves over to our new Owner. We are giving Him control of our whole life and saying to Him, 'I am yours'.

Such a transaction is very big, far bigger than the car or house used in our illustration. It is your whole person! Isn't it good to know that the new Owner is able to keep safely what we commit to Him? He will **never** lose us!

Listen to what God's Word says: 'Being confident of this, that He who began a good work in you will carry it on to completion until the day of Christ Jesus.' AND 'I know whom I have believed, and am convinced that He is able to guard what I have entrusted to Him for that day.' (Philippians 1:6, 2 Timothy 1:12.) He will keep you totally. You are also saying to Him, 'I give you total control over every area of my life; what I do; what I shall be; who I marry; how I use my time, money and everything else.' Can you think of any area of your life that should not be under His control?

....

Baptism then has great significance: it is a definite finishing with the old life and an entry into a commitment to the Lord Jesus which will last throughout your life. It is like having a 'big bath' in the name of the Lord! Indeed you can thank Him as you are being baptised for the washing away of all your past sin (Acts 22:16).

Of course if you have no **inner experience** of these things, all that will happen is that you will get wet! But if there is true faith and a real heart knowledge then your baptism will be a valid and glorious expression and experience of these truths.

Having carefully and prayerfully considered what the Bible teaches about baptism will you write down very briefly your response to God's Word, indicating whether you are willing to be baptised by immersion when this can be arranged?

....

....

SOME PRACTICAL INFORMATION ABOUT A BAPTISMAL SERVICE

Obviously the details and circumstances of a baptismal service will change from place to place but these comments will be of general guidance.

1. The baptism may take place at the end of a service or during a time of worship. The leader or leaders baptising you will go down into the pool first. You will then join them and your family and friends, or in some places the whole church, will gather round the pool so that they are all able to share in the joy and glory of what is happening.

2. It is often helpful for the church, visiting friends, family and so on, to know that the one who is being baptised is clearly rejoicing in what God has done in his or her life. So you will probably be asked, 'Have you turned from your sins and believed on the Lord Jesus?' or a similar kind of question. You can then respond to that as briefly or as fully as you wish!

3. You will then be baptised - in the name of the Father, Son and Holy Spirit (or some similar words). SPLASH!

4. When you are brought up out of the water, those who have baptised you may well want to remain in the pool so that they can pray for you. This is often a good time to ask God to pour out His Spirit upon you or to commend you especially to God in prayer. They will want your baptism to be, not a rushed 'in and out' affair, but an occasion for you to enjoy and remember.

5. You can then leave the pool and either wait to see the baptisms of any others being baptised with you, or go to another room to change before rejoining the service.

6. You will need to bring with you a towel and a bag to put your wet things in. Men should wear an open-necked shirt and trousers. Ladies may wear a long dress (weighted round the hem), or a blouse and long skirt or jeans.

NB Don't forget to bring some fresh underwear to change into afterwards.

In our next lesson we shall look at another kind of baptism - baptism in the Holy Spirit.

Lesson 4
BAPTISM IN THE HOLY SPIRIT

Scriptures to read before this lesson	
Day 1	Luke 24:13-53
Day 2	Acts1:1-11
Day 3	1 Corinthians 14:1-28
Day 4	1 Corinthianss 12:1-31
Day 5	1 Corinthians 2:1-16
Day 6	Galatians 5:13-26
Day 7	Luke 11:1-13

THE CHRISTIAN LIFE IS A SUPERNATURAL LIFE

From our parents we received natural life, but in order to become Christians we needed a 'birth from God' - the results of which we looked at in Lesson 2. We then saw that there is a baptism in water which cuts us off from the old life and unites us with Jesus in His resurrection.

In this lesson we are going to see how God supernaturally and powerfully equips us to serve Him. Almost everyone has these very common fears about the Christian faith and becoming a follower of Jesus.

I won't be able to keep it up.
I'll never be able to tell anyone about the Lord Jesus.
I'm sure I shall be a failure.

All of these fears were experienced by the disciples. But just before Jesus ascended to His Father He promised them something. We will look at the Scriptures and see what it was:-

Look up Luke 24:49 and write down what Jesus promised would happen to the disciples.

They would be ....

Turn to Acts 1:4-5 and write down the gift the Father promised:

....

Now look at Acts 1:8 and write down what they would receive when the Holy Spirit came upon them:

....

What would this enable them to be? ....

So then, this promised gift of the Holy Spirit (sometimes called 'the baptism in the Spirit') would empower them and equip them to serve the Lord Jesus. Was it for those first disciples only, or for all of God's children?

Look up Acts 2:38-39

Write out verse 39 ....

....

....

Do you qualify? YES/NO

WHO IS THE HOLY SPIRIT?

The Holy Spirit is not 'it', an impersonal force or power, but a divine person. He is a member of the Godhead - Father, Son and Holy Spirit - and He shares the same nature as the Father and the Son and is to be worshipped and glorified with them. He is the gift of the Father and the Son to the Christian so that He can live within us and give us spiritual life (John 3:5-8). As He becomes our Strengthener and Helper, He enables us to live the Christian life fully. The Holy Spirit didn't just come on the scene on Whit Sunday or Pentecost but was always with the Father and the Son. He was involved:

in creation - see Genesis 1:1, 2
in producing the Scriptures and prophecy- see 2 Peter 1:20, 21
in equipping and strengthening God's people in Old Testament times - see Exodus 31:3-5 and Judges 14:6

But in the Old Testament the prophets always seemed to be longing for the day when He would come in fulness on all the people of God- see Joel 2:28,29. That's what happened on that first Whit Sunday: it was the start of a 'new age', the age of the outpoured Holy Spirit, as we shall go on to see.

WHAT IS THE BAPTISM IN THE HOLY SPIRIT?

We cannot be holy without the Holy Spirit. We cannot truly serve without Him. We cannot be sure that we are God's children without Him. We need more than a set of rules, or a head knowledge of Christian teaching. We saw from Lesson 3 that baptism means to 'immerse' or 'overwhelm'. To be baptised in water is to be totally immersed - to get thoroughly wet! To be baptised in the Holy Spirit is to be thoroughtly immersed in the Holy Spirit - that is why being baptised in the Holy Spirit is described in the Bible in a number of ways, such as 'being clothed with', 'coming upon', 'outpouring', 'filled with' or 'falling upon'. There is a variety of expression because people experience His coming in different ways, but it all adds up to a very definite experience of receiving the Holy Spirit.

WHAT DOES THE HOLY SPIRIT DO IN US AND FOR US?

1. As we have seen, Jesus promised that we would receive power when the Holy Spirit comes upon us - power to be witnesses. A witness is someone who testifies to the truth about someone or something. The Holy Spirit will help us to **live** and **speak** in such a way that people will know that we are different - that we are 'Jesus people'. What happened in Acts 4:31 when the people were filled with the Holy Spirit?

They ....

2. Look up Romans 8:14-16. What does the Holy Spirit do in us?

....

He testifies (to 'declare and establish as a fact') with our spirit that we are God's children. His coming upon us is a 'seal' securing us as God's possession for ever (Ephesians 1:13,14). The baptism in the Holy Spirit is described in Romans 5:5 as God pouring out His love into our hearts - this makes for a wonderfully close and secure relationship with our Heavenly Father. It is to **experience** God's love within us.

3. We shall be able to pray and sing with the help of the Holy Spirit, not only with our minds and in our usual language of English, but from our spirits and with a language given by the Holy Spirit - see 1 Corinthians 14:15. This 'praying with my spirit' is the same as 'praying in a tongue'. Because it is important to understand what the Scriptures teach about this we will look at it more fully in the later part of the lesson.

4. The Holy Spirit is the One who equips God's people for all kinds of service and worship in the church. We do not need great intellect or natural talents - we need the Holy Spirit of God!
Look at 1 Corinthians 12:4-11 and write down the various ways in which the Holy Spirit equips God's people - there are nine mentioned in this passage.

a) ....

b) ....

c) ....

d) ....

e) ....

f) ....

g) ....

h) ....

i) ....

Now go back over the list and put a tick against any that you have either seen or heard being used in the church.

5. The Holy Spirit helps us to understand the words and thoughts of God. Look at 1 Corinthians 2:8-13. Write down briefly in your **own** words the main thrust of what the passage is saying.

....

....

....

6. The Holy Spirit does for us what the Lord Jesus did for the disciples - He was with them to teach them how to live God's life. The Holy Spirit comes into us to do the same. As we live our daily lives the Holy Spirit will teach us to say 'NO' to sin and ungodliness, and to say 'YES' to God and righteousness. Jesus spoke of this as 'taking up the cross' - the cross means death. Following the desires of the sinful nature is letting those desires 'live'; **not** following them is 'putting them to death'. Do you remember reading about this in Galatians 5:13-26? If we 'live in the Spirit' He will enable us to live a very different kind of life from that which we used to live.
What sort of 'fruit' will He produce in our lives? Write it down:

....

....

....

HOW DOES ONE RECEIVE THE BAPTISM IN THE HOLY SPIRIT?

Let us look at several examples in the Scriptures of how the Spirit was received. Jot down the key facts in each case.

	KEY FACTS
1. The Lord Jesus. 'When all the people were being baptised, Jesus was baptised too. And as he was praying heaven was opened and the	....

Holy Spirit descended on him in bodily form like a dove. And a voice came from heaven. "You are my Son, whom I love; with you I am well pleased. "' Luke 3:21, 22.

....

....

....

2. The 120 disciples. 'All of them were filled with the Holy Spirit and began to speak in other tongues as the Spirit enabled them.' Acts 2:4

....

....

3. The centurion's household. 'While Peter was still speaking these words, the Holy Spirit came on all who heard the message. The circumcised believers (Jewish Christians) who had come with Peter were astonised that the gift of the Holy Spirit had been poured out even on the Gentiles. For they heard them speaking in tongues and praising God.' Acts 10:44-46

....

....

....

....

....

....

4. The Ephesians. ' ... they were baptised into the name of the Lord Jesus. When Paul placed his hand on them, the Holy Spirit came on them, and they spoke in tongues and prophesied.' Acts 19:5-6

....

....

....

5. The promise of Jesus. 'Jesus said, "If anyone is thirsty, let him come to me and drink. Whoever believes in me, as the Scripture has said, streams of living water will flow from within him." By this he meant the Spirit...' John 7:37-39.

....

....

....

....

These five passages indicate that there is no set pattern for the receiving of the Holy Spirit. However certain things are very evident:

1. A longing and a thirst which causes you to ask.
2. A coming to the Lord in faith.
3. A moment of receiving the Spirit and being filled.
4. A responding in worship, praise and usually tongues.

It is very important that you **ask** God for the gift of the Holy Spirit. Look at Luke 11:11-13. **Look it up.** Being filled or baptised in the Holy Spirit is not complicated. It means coming to God with faith and receiving what God has promised and then simply letting God do it! You then need to respond (indeed you will!) by praising God with your whole heart, opening your mouth and speaking the words which come from deep within. Don't be afraid of emotion - being baptised in the Spirit will affect your whole inner being and personality.

There is no set time for this, but if you are really thirsty you won't want to delay asking; it could be at the time of your being baptised in water. In that case those who baptise you will lay hands on you and pray with you.

SPEAKING IN TONGUES

This is speaking in a language which you have not learnt but which is given by the Holy Spirit. He does this in order that you can worship, praise, pray or intercede (pray for others) very freely from deep within your spirit in words which He gives. You will not understand the words you speak for they do not come from your mind but your spirit.

Because it is not 'natural' to speak words which you do not understand you may at first find yourself thinking, 'I'm making this up' - this is not an unusual reaction! The answer to this is to believe what God says in His Word - speaking in tongues is a gift of the Holy Spirit. It is perfectly normal for Spirit-baptised Christians to speak in tongues. You are encouraged, too, to ask the Holy Spirit to give you the interpretation of your praying. You will probably find when you pray in English afterwards that God will give you the understanding of what you had previously prayed (See 1 Corinthians 14:13).

Praying in tongues or singing praise to God in tongues will usually be a part of your personal praying and fellowshipping with God. If you exercise the gift in a gathering of God's people then it will need interpreting, either by someone else who has the gift of interpretation, or, if this does not happen, by your praying and asking God to give you the interpretation.

NB. What should you do if nothing happens when you pray or when someone prays for you to be baptised in the Holy Spirit? Don't just leave it; there will be a reason. Make a point of seeing your course leader so that you can talk about it together.

ANY QUESTIONS? ....

....

....

....

....

....

....

This is the last lesson in the part of the course dealing with becoming a Christian. The second part of the teaching course is concerned with becoming a member of the church.

Part Two

BECOMING A MEMBER OF THE CHURCH

Becoming a Christian and becoming part of the church of Christ are inseparably linked together in the Scriptures and therefore should be in our experience too.

In Acts 2 those who repented of their sin and believed on the Lord Jesus at the preaching of Peter were baptised and filled with the Holy Spirit. We then go on to read that 'they were added to the number of believers and they devoted themselves to the apostles' teaching, fellowship, breaking of bread and prayers'.

In this second part of the Basic Teaching Course we are going to look at what it means to be 'added to the church'.

Please follow the pattern of Part 1 by reading the relevant passages from the Scriptures day by day prior to the lesson.

Daily readings prior to the lessons

	Lesson 5	**Lesson 6**	**Lesson 7**
Day 1	Acts 2:40-47	Romans 12:1-21	Heb. 10:19-25
Day 2	Ephesians 4:1-16	Matthew 18:15-22	Luke 22:7-20
Day 3	1 Timothy 3:1-16	James 2:1-17	1 Cor. 11:23-34
Day 4	1 Peter 5:1-11	1 Cor. 14:26-33	1 Thess. 1:1-10
Day 5	Acts 6:1-17	Ephesians 4:17-32	2 Cor. 9:6-15
Day 6	Acts 13:1-12	Luke 9:10-17	Proverbs 3:1-10
Day 7	Acts 14:1-27	Ephesians 5:21-6:9	Romans 15:1-13

Lesson 5
LEARNING ABOUT THE CHURCH

Scriptures to read before this lesson
Day 1 Acts 2:40-47
Day 2 Ephesians 4:1-16
Day 3 1 Timothy 3:1-16
Day 4 1 Peter 5:1-11
Day 5 Acts 6:1-7
Day 6 Acts 13:1-12
Day 7 Acts 14:1-27

A

B

"They devoted themselves to the apostles' teaching and to fellowship, to the breaking of bread and to prayer. Everyone was filled with awe, and many wonders and miraculous signs were done by the apostles. All the believers were together and had everything in common. Selling their possessions and goods, they gave to anyone as he had need. Every day they continued to meet together in the temple courts. They broke bread in their homes and ate together with glad and sincere hearts, praising God and enjoying the favour of all the people. And the Lord added to their number daily those who were being saved."
Acts 2:42-47

WHICH IS THE CHURCH - A or B?

The church of the New Testament was not a building at the corner of the road, but God's redeemed people gathered together, properly taught and shepherded, loving and serving the Lord and each other, and being a blessing to the community in which they lived.

The New Testament says nothing about times of church services, organisations, by which name a church should be called, or its architecture. But it does have a great deal to say about the people of which it is comprised and the quality of love and life that should be present: it speaks about leadership, discipline, serving, giving, unity, praying, teaching and many other topics.

In this lesson, we shall be looking at some of these vital aspects of a church's life.

A STRUCTURED CHURCH

Over the centuries the church has been broken, fragmented and divided into many denominations so that in most towns there are numbers of different churches, all too often having little to do with each other. This was not so in New Testament times. The church was united and was one in doctrine, life and practice, despite the fact that it existed in many different countries, cultures and nationalities in the towns and cities of the Near and Middle East.

When we read the letters of the apostles we can see that there were problems: there were pressures from self-seeking individuals; error needed to be refuted and corrected; and false teachers and teaching had to be challenged. Nevertheless the church was essentially one.

How was this unity preserved? It was preserved through the ministries of the Lord Jesus.

EPHESIANS 4 MINISTRIES

When the Lord Jesus ascended into heaven He gave to His church apostles, prophets, evangelists, pastors and teachers. Read Ephesians 4:11-13 and note the word **until** in verse 13. What time does that word refer to?

....

....

Do you think that we have reached that yet? YES/NO

Clearly the answer is 'NO'. These ascension gifts of Christ are obviously of tremendous importance so it is worth spending some time looking at what they are. Most people are familiar with terms like bishop, cardinal, curate, minister, pope, priest, rector, vicar and so on, but many of these are not mentioned in Scripture and result from centuries of confusion throughout the church's history. This only serves to emphasize the importance of returning to the 'norm' of the Bible.

Let us look then at these ministries mentioned in Ephesians 4.

Apostles

The New Testament shows us what a key role the apostles had in the building of the church. Their ministry was foundational. Over the centuries the teaching has emerged that apostles were only present in the church in its early years. However, the Bible does not teach that. Some thought that there were only twelve apostles and that the apostle Paul replaced Judas. However, the Bible does not say that and we do notice that Bamabas (Acts 14:14), James, the brother of Jesus (1 Corinthians 15:7), Andronicus and Junias (Romans 16:7) and others are referred to as apostles in the New Testament.

Every ministry that men receive is a gift of God. It is not something attained through human skill. Paul describes his apostolic ministry as follows: 'By the grace God has given me, I laid a foundation as an expert builder.' Perhaps this is the clearest description of apostolic ministry in the Bible. He sees the church at Corinth as proof of his apostleship - in other words, the fact that a church had been planted and established was proof of his ability to build. The apostles also usually had an ongoing relationship with the churches, such as that which Paul writes about in 1 Thessalonians 3:10.

His foundation laying had four main aspects:

Planting new churches. The word 'apostle' means 'one clothed with the authority and endued with the power of the Sender'. (Norval Geldenhuys, *Supreme Authority*).The apostles recognised that in a special way they were 'sent forth' by Jesus to propagate new churches. This is an important part of apostolic ministry.

Doctrinal teaching. Paul made sure that people were firmly rooted in Christ, declaring to them the mysteries of Christ (Ephesians 3:5). He brought corrective teaching if the churches began to drift away from the truth (the letter to the Galatian church is an example of this).

Conduct. He made sure that their life-style was in keeping with the teaching they had been given (1 Thessalonians 4:1-2).

Eldership appointment. The elders in local churches were not 'self-appointed' leaders - the churches had the security of having men appointed either by the apostles (Acts 14:23) or those delegated by them - eg. Titus (Titus 1:5)

Today, when God is restoring His church, one of the major apostolic functions will be that of bringing the church back onto its right foundations.

Prophets

These are men who usually work alongside the apostles and they, together with the apostles, are involved in laying foundations (Ephesians 2:20). Prophets give direction and encouragement to the churches and because they are 'see-ers' their ministry helps to give insight and understanding about the things God wants done in the Church. There are times when this can be quite disturbing especially when the issues may be 'dead traditions' or long-standing unresolved conflicts and problems; nevertheless we need that provoking ministry of the prophet.

Evangelists

These men have special ability from God to preach the gospel very powerfully and bring people to salvation. Philip is an example of a man with such an evangelistic ministry (see Acts chapter 8). You will notice he preached to many as well as to an individual; often this was accompanied by miraculous signs such as healings and deliverance. This ministry, as with all the others in Ephesians 4, is primarily to the church and is designed to 'prepare God's people for works of service'.

How would an evangelist do this, do you suppose? ....

....

....

Pastors

The Greek word means 'SHEPHERD' - the Eastern shepherd led the flock by going in front of the sheep; seeking good pasture, giving protection, wisely caring for the whole flock. Ezekiel 34 contains a very full description of this function. The Lord Jesus is **the** example of this shepherding care - see John chapter 10.

Teachers

These are men who are responsible for giving teaching and instruction. The Christian life is not a 'do-it-yourself' religion. God has spoken. He has given us clear commands to be obeyed. There are principles for living godly lives which need to be put into practice. Whilst it is true that when we become Christians the Holy Spirit writes God's laws on our hearts (Hebrews 8:10) nevertheless we all need re-educating! We need teaching about life, money, love, family, work, worship, relationships, our origins and destiny and more.

These last two ministries of pastor and teacher are so closely linked that it is possible that both are combined in the same person. We might as easily speak of a pastor/teacher. It is impossible to tell from the Greek text whether they are separate or combined ministries.

Normally men in all these categories, whilst perhaps having a specially close relationship with a local church, would have a sphere of influence far wider than that - this would be especially true of apostles, prophets and evangelists - and all would probably work in a team setting with the apostle. It is this ministry described in Ephesians 4 which brings order, direction, strength, growth and unity to the local churches.

Let us sum it up by asking 'Who is head of the church?' ....

.... (Ephesians 1:22-23)

How is this headship and authority exercised? ....

....

The Lord Jesus exercises His authority and care for His people through these ministries of apostles, prophets, evangelists, pastors and

teachers. See how He fulfils these ministries Himself as well as giving them to His church.
Look up these references and write against each one the appropriate 'gift' from Ephesians 4:11.

Heb 3:1 .... John 10:11 .... Acts 3:22 ....

Luke 4:18 ....John 13:13 ....

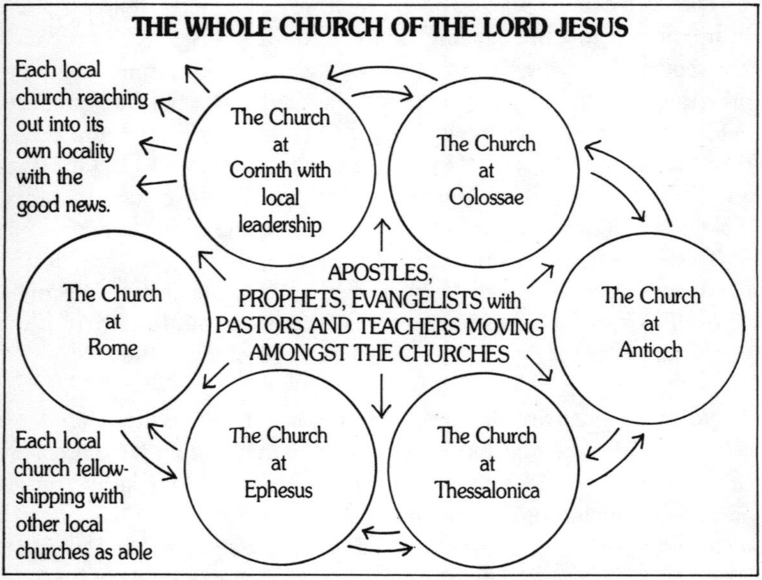

It is this kind of church which God is restoring in these days and this is happening all over the world. Many local churches are seeking to follow this New Testament pattern and to recognise and work with similar churches, acknowledging and receiving true apostolic and prophetic ministry.

LOCAL CHURCH STRUCTURE

As we have seen in the diagram and in the Scriptures that you have been reading prior to this lesson there is a difference between churches in a locality and the whole church of Christ which is made up of all believers everywhere.

WHAT IS A LOCAL CHURCH?

Local churches are situated in towns and areas where believers living in the same neighbourhood can come together to form a congregation under properly constituted leadership. The local church does not include everyone who attends a place of worship. It comprises only those who have been truly converted to God (that involves all that we have seen in the first part of the course) and are committed to each other and to God's appointed leadership to form a 'body of Christ' in a locality (that is what this second part is all about).

WHO ARE THE LEADERS AND HOW ARE THEY APPOINTED?

The Lord Jesus is head of the church - the Bible is quite clear about this. There is no earthly or human head. Having said this, the church is not a 'free-for-all' - that would lead to chaos! The Lord Himself has given authority to men to rule and shepherd His flock - He himself provides such men for His church. In practice this means that God raises up from among the congregation a man of spiritual gift and ability who has a loving and caring heart and a real desire to serve God's people. This is recognised by the church and the man set forth for this ministry of service by the laying on of hands of other leaders - see Acts 6:1-6, Acts 13:3, Acts 14:23 and Titus 1:5.

In many circles such leaders have been recognised and appointed in order that they might serve the Lord and His people. There are:

Elders

These men are responsible for the whole church and its teaching, spiritual oversight, pastoral care and discipline. Some of these elders may be in full time service. The elders have authority and oversight of the church. Because their role is primarily to do with government and authority we believe this should be exercised by men - see 1 Timothy 2:11. In order to carry out this ministry the elders need the help of others. Those who help in this way are:

Deacons

The word 'deacon' means 'one who serves'. There are many practical and pastoral matters in church life where able men and women can serve the elders in areas like administration, finance, maintenance of buildings and visitation of elderly or sick people. In larger churches there may need to be small teams of people involved - thus giving opportunity for many to serve one another in love. (Indeed the whole church should be a serving church!) Those heading up such teams would have a deaconing function.

Housegroup Leaders

They also come into this category, for they too serve the elders in having responsibility for the care and discipling of small groups of people in the church.

HOW IS THEIR MINISTRY TO BE EXERCISED?

This is not to be in a crushing and overbearing manner, but in the same way as the Lord Jesus. Look at these two Scriptures:

2 Corinthians 10:8 '... the authority the Lord gave us for **building you up** rather than **pulling you down** ...'

1 Peter 5:2,3 'Be shepherds of God's flock that is under your care, serving as overseers - not because you must, but because you are willing, as God wants you to be; not greedy for money, but eager to serve; not lording it over those entrusted to you, but being examples to the flock.'

It is this kind of leadership that God wants in His church. Such leaders are to:

Shepherd - that is to feed, protect and lead.
Rule - that is to exercise godly discipline.
Oversee - that is to watch over the people's lives, their doctrine and so on.
Serve - that is to give help in practical and spiritual things.
Be an example - that is to live open, transparent lives that others can follow.

WHAT KIND OF RESPONSE WILL GOD REQUIRE OF THOSE WHO ARE MEMBERS OF HIS CHURCH?

Let us look at three Scriptures. Pick out the key words which show what that response should be.

1 Timothy 5:17 'The elders who direct the affairs of the church well are worthy of double honour, especially those whose work is preaching and teaching.'

1 Thessalonians 5:12-13 'Now we ask you, brothers, to respect those who work hard among you, who are over you in the Lord and who admonish you. Hold them in the highest regard in love because of their work.'

Hebrews 13:17 'Obey your leaders and submit to their authority. They keep watch over you as men who must give an account. Obey them so that their work will be a joy, not a burden, for that would be of no advantage to you. '

This is **not** a 'big-stick' authority. God wants His people to receive and benefit from the ministries He has set in the church. As in a well-ordered family, authority is to be there not to suppress the children or destroy their initiative, but to help them grow up into full maturity and responsible adulthood.

Because, as we saw in Lesson 3, Jesus' lordship extends to every area of our lives, we would hope that you would want those in leadership to extend their care toward you and your whole life. The Lord Jesus calls us to submit to His word and to obey His teaching with a heart of humility and love. This is how we grow in the Christian life.

The church is not a two-tier structure of leaders and members - it is family. It is a body in which every part is important. God has nevertheless given different functions and gifts to different parts of the body. When we belong to God's church we need to love and serve one another. There is a mutual care and discipling (the process by which we become mature Christians) which must take place alongside that which is done by those in leadership.

To become part of the church, then, means to receive and accept the ministry of God's shepherds and leaders.

Do you see the rightness of this kind of discipling? ....
Are there any areas of your life that you feel should be excluded from the godly and wise care, correction and help of God's appointed shepherds?

....

....

....

The next lesson deals with different aspects of our life together in the church.

Lesson 6
LIFE IN THE CHURCH

Scriptures to read before this lesson
Day 1 Romans 12:1-21
Day 2 Matthew 18:15-22
Day 3 James 2:1-17
Day 4 1 Corinthians 14:26-33
Day 5 Ephesians 4:17-32
Day 6 Luke 9:10-17
Day 7 Ephesians 5:21 - 6:9

In this lesson we are going to look at three important areas of our life together: our mutual responsibilities to each other, housegroups, and our relationship with the Lord Jesus.

LOVING, SERVING AND CARING FOR EACH OTHER

In the previous lesson we learnt about leadership; this was necessary but it is only a part of the whole. One of the beautiful word-pictures of the church is that of 'family'. The church is God's family and within that family there are great privileges and responsibilities. In this lesson we will learn what some of these are.

1. Building each other up through the exercise of a spiritual gift

(1 Corinthians 14:26-29, Romans 12:3-8). These verses tell us that we can build up and strengthen each other by bringing a prophecy, a hymn, a tongue or a word of instruction. Each member of the church needs to be encouraged to seek God for such spiritual gifts and to use

them in church gatherings and housegroups. Building others up is not just for leaders - it's the responsibility and privilege of every member.

Do you know what your spiritual gift may be? If so, write it down.

....

2. Practical acts of kindness and service

There are many ways in which we can serve one another: visiting those who are sick, lonely or elderly and practising hospitality (Romans 12:9-13). Within the church there are often things that need doing (typing, baking, painting, electrical repairs and so on). Do you have any practical abilities which may be of service to God's people?

What are they?...

....

The church of Jesus is a family and we are to preserve the family unity; see Romans 12:14-18. If you have something against another brother or sister, you are to seek prayerfully to put it right - Matthew 18:15-17. We are not to gossip about each other or the church, neither to those inside nor outside the church. Our speech and relationships are very important (Ephesians 4:1-6 and 29-32).

3. Ministering to each other in practical needs

The church is a family and members should be able to count on the loving care of their brothers and sisters. We are to take seriously the examples in James 2.

HOUSEGROUPS

Twenty years ago few churches would have known what was meant by this term. Not so in New Testament times when it was a frequent practice of Christians to meet in homes for breaking of bread, teaching, fellowship and prayer (Acts 2:46, 12:12, 16:40; Romans 16:4, 5, 23; 1 Cor. 16:19 and so on). It is clear in the Scriptures that God has provided a variety of different levels at which His people should meet and relate together. Moses, for example, realised that he couldn't govern an entire nation on his own and therefore divided the people into units of ten upwards (Exodus 18:13-27). The Lord Jesus could teach over five thousand people, but when it came to meeting their physical needs He commanded that they sit in groups of fifty. The apostles could then ensure that everyone was fed! (Luke 9:12-17). The early church had its large congregational gatherings but, as is evident from the references above, it also often met in homes.

1. The purpose of housegroups

It is obvious that one pastor (or even two or three) cannot adequately care for, visit, personally counsel or individually teach a church of even a moderate size; nor could all the members know each other in depth. So many churches have divided the people into smaller units of about twelve to twenty which meet during the week in the home of an 'under shepherd' or housegroup leader. The housegroup leaders exercise a spiritual care of the people in their groups and work with and under the Pastors and Elders. Some of the main objectives of housegroups are listed below:

a. To work out, apply and go over the teaching given in the larger congregational gatherings. The vital 'Did you understand?' 'How should we put the teaching into practice?' type of question can be asked and answered.

b. God's people can develop and exercise spiritual gifts in the smaller and less daunting atmosphere of a home. Encouragement can be given to begin praying aloud, sharing an experience and more.

c. There can be a much greater level of care for the practical needs of each person.

d. In a large congregation it is very easy to be lost in the crowd or even to opt out, but in a smaller committed group with people of different ages and backgrounds it is possible to receive love and serve each other. It is this kind of deep relationship and caring that makes for real growth.

e. A housegroup is like a small 'combat unit' able to carry out specific functions which a larger congregation could not easily do. The group can also take specific prayer needs of individuals, missionaries and others and pray them through.

2. How to participate in a housegroup.

The basis of all our church life is commitment and relationship.

Firstly this is to the Lord Himself, then it is to those whom He has placed over you to 'shepherd' you. Ideally your housegroup leader and his wife will be available to you and will want you to feel that you can share any needs or problems with them. The housegroup is not to be thought of as a place you go to once a week BUT as the committed relationship you have with your under-shepherd and your brothers and sisters. This means that you must be willing to attend regularly and to receive counsel and teaching. God's aim for us is that we come to mature Christian growth.

Be prepared! Go to the group having spent some time in prayer first.

Be open to God! Generally the housegroup will be worship and teaching centred. Be sensitive to the Holy Spirit's leading - you may be prompted to pray, to introduce a song, or to share an experience.

Be open to each other! One of the purposes of the smaller unit is to love and serve, encourage and help each other. Don't be shy, seek to go out to people.

Be yourself! God wants you to be real. Learn to talk to God naturally. Be real about sharing your needs and other aspects of your life.

Be committed! Generally, any group activity means submission of the individual need to the common need or good of the whole. If you are really committed you will not find that difficult. Be loyal.

Be regular! The housegroup is not 'just another meeting'. It is one of the means God has ordained for your spiritual growth (See Hebrews 10:23-25).

THE IMPORTANCE OF GROWING IN THE FAITH AND THE KNOWLEDGE OF THE LORD JESUS

We have been stressing throughout this lesson our life together in the church. But it is vitally important that each member individually grows in the knowledge of God. There is no better way than by:

1. Regularly attending the church gatherings for worship and teaching.

We have already seen the importance of this.

2. Spending time with the Lord in personal prayer and worship.

True prayer is the secret of the Christian life and the key to your fellowship with God. If you do not pray, then your Christian life will soon become a dull, lifeless chore. You need to see that there is a difference between saying prayers and true praying. Praying is not simply repeating the same old words day after day nor doing a religious duty; it is speaking to God and as time goes on, sensing that He is speaking to You; it is a conversation with your heavenly Father.

Praying aloud can be a wonderful remedy for 'wandering thoughts' - **talk** to God about everything - your family, your work, your desires and so on. **Praise** Him for His care of you and for being part of His church. **Worship** Him for His greatness, His creation, His gift of salvation. **Ask** Him to make you a man or woman of God, to help you share your faith with others and to make you grow as a Christian. Don't feel you have to use 'religious' language. Be yourself.

3. Reading the Scriptures and thinking upon His Word.

If you are a new Christian you must not expect that you will understand everying at once! The Bible is a big book and it does take time for God's truth to sink in. You will grow most rapidly in understanding as you learn to obey that truth which you have been able to grasp. Do not be discouraged, for God wants you to grow in understanding - Hebrews 5:12-14. Is there anything in your reading of the Bible so far that you haven't understood?

....

....

....

God's Word is as needful to us as daily food. It is meant to become part of our being, absorbed into our personalities so much that our very thoughts and speech are 'Christlike' (Psalm 119:11, Deuteronomy 11:18-21). You will, therefore, need to deliberately set aside a time each day to read the Scriptures. If you have not read the Bible before, a good starting point is Luke's Gospel followed by the Acts of the Apostles. This will give you a basic knowledge of the Lord Jesus Christ, His life, teaching, death and resurrection, the birth and growth of the church plus a very brief survey of the Old Testament (in Acts 7).

It would be a good plan to read one chapter a day, asking God to teach you and build you up in your faith and love for Him. Come to Him in prayer and ask Him to reveal Himself to you as you read - remember the Scriptures are a revelation of God.

4. Doing the will of God in your home, family life and daily work.

The Christian life means a new lifestyle! The Scriptures give an entirely different view of the importance and value of relationships and responsibilities within marriage, family and even in our work. Read through Ephesians 5:21-6:9. In what ways do these verses set out different attitudes from contemporary ones regarding:

marriage ....

....

parents ....

....

children ....

....

work (the passage refers to masters and slaves but there are principles which still apply)

....

....?

> **Do you feel that you need special help in any of the above?**
>
> If so, please indicate which area so that your group leader can talk this over with you.
>
> ....
>
> ....

Our final lesson will deal with some specific issues related to 'joining the family' of God's people.

Lesson 7
JOINING THE FAMILY

Scriptures to read before this lesson	
Day 1	Hebrews 10:19-25
Day 2	Luke 22:7-20
Day3	1 Corinthians 11:23-34
Day 4	1 Thessalonians 1:1-10
Day 5	2 Corinthians 9:6-15
Day 6	Proverbs 3:1-10
Day 7	Romans 15:1-13

In this lesson we are going to look at the Lord's Supper, giving to the Lord's work, spreading the good news and becoming a member of the church.

THE LORD'S SUPPER

For the sake of new Christians it may be helpful to say a little about this wonderful, though simple, meal that Christians have shared in for nearly two thousand years. You will have read about it in Luke 22:7-20 and 1 Corinthians 11:23-24. This meal usually forms part of the worshipping life of God's people when they gather on the Lord's Day or perhaps in a housegroup. There is no rigid pattern or order laid down in Scripture - the emphasis is not on the way in which the ceremony is conducted but on the state of our hearts and lives. There are four key words which will help to explain what the Lord's Supper is:

Remembrance

Jesus said, 'Do this in remembrance of Me'. He is the most important person present. We are to remember (think about) His great love and sacrifice for our sins at Calvary. The **broken** bread and **poured out** wine are vivid pictures of His sufferings for us. Notice how personal it is.

Luke 22:19 ' .... body given for ....'

Luke 22:20 ' .... blood which is poured out for ....'

Covenant

The word speaks of a promise which cannot be broken. The blood of the new covenant tells us that God's promise to save, forgive and redeem His believing people will **never** be broken. We, on our part, need to see ourselves as God's covenant people - and to live righteously. It is a serious matter to take the Lord's Supper. See what happened when some of the early Christians became careless and wilfully went on sinning (1 Corinthians 11:30, 31).

Fellowship

The Lord's Supper is a meal that God's people eat **together**. Communion ('koinonia' in Greek) means 'sharing together': it is a family meal. That is why we share the one loaf - it reminds us that we belong to each other (and to Him). We are **together** in Christ. We need therefore to examine our hearts to make sure that that is so in reality. We need to enjoy being together and to express our love to each other.

Hope

Are we to eat this meal for ever? Look up 1 Corinthians 11:26.

It is until ....

One day we will see Jesus 'face to face.' Until then we feed upon Him in this 'spiritual meal'.

GIVING TO THE LORD AND HIS WORK

It is obvious from even a quick reading of the Scriptures that God has a lot to say about money. Money itself is not evil. It is the **love** of money that is the root of all evil (1 Timothy 6:10). Jesus said that the way a man handled his money was an indication of whether he could be trusted with true spiritual riches (Luke 16:10,11).

It is evident that in the Kingdom of God money is important. God's servants need to be released from spending all their time in secular employment so that they can devote themselves fully to the work of ministry. Evangelism, outreach and especially spreading the gospel throughout the world and projects amongst the socially deprived require large sums of money. Needs amongst the people of God are to be met. The poor are to be cared for. Church buildings need to be heated and maintained. God's way of meeting these needs is through the giving of His people - it was so in both the Old and the New Testaments.

Let us look at some general New Testament principles:

2 Corinthians 8:3 'They gave **as much as they were able**, and even beyond their ability. Entirely on their own' (i.e. of their own free will).

2 Corinthians 9:7 'Each man should give **what he has decided in his heart** to give, not reluctantly or under compulsion, for God loves a **cheerful** giver'.

1 Corinthians 16:2 'On the first day of every week, each of you should set aside a sum of money **in keeping with his income**...'

Luke 6:38 '**Give, and it will be given to you**. A good measure, pressed down, shaken together and running over, will be poured into your lap. For with the measure you use, it will be measured to you.'

Clearly God intends our giving to be:

1. In proportion to our means

2. With willingness and cheerfulness

3. Systematic, rather than haphazard

4. With faith, believing God will supply our needs as we give.

In the Old Testament the Israelites gave a 'tithe' (a tenth) of their incomes for the support of the religious leaders, the Levites, so that they could be free to concentrate on their spiritual ministries in the tabernacle and in teaching the people of God. And whilst tithing is not specifically commended in the New Testament it does serve as a guide to the general level of giving that we should be considering. In days of financial difficulty one may be tempted not to give, but God has established a principle of faith: 'Give and it shall be given to you.'

Here are some of the things the giving of the Lord's people may be used for in a church:

To pay the salaries of the full-time pastor(s).

To finance evangelistic and apostolic outreach at home and abroad.

To minister to those who have financial needs.

To maintain the church buildings.

To cover the cost of such items as stationery, postage, heating, lighting and so on.

From time to time some churches take up special offerings for specific purposes.

If you have any questions about giving or the use of money, please feel free to ask your group leader. Many churches have a covenanting scheme whereby the church is able to recover the tax paid by the donors on their gifts. Details of this may be obtained from the church treasurer. There are great advantages in this scheme: it enables you, simply and privately, to make more cash available to the church with the tax man's blessing.

SPREADING THE GOOD NEWS

Do you remember the diagram of the churches in lesson 5? It showed each church reaching out into its locality with the good news. This is a vital part of true church life. In Acts 2:42-47 an outstanding feature of the Jerusalem church was that 'the Lord added to their number daily those who were being saved'.

For what does the apostle Paul commend the church at Thessalonica? Look up 1 Thessalonians 1:7-9 and write it down.

....

....

It is in this way that people are saved and other churches started. We have a responsibility to reproduce and multiply. God's purpose is both local and world-wide; the whole earth is to be 'filled with the knowledge of the Lord'. Individually and as local churches we are to share in this great purpose.

How?

1. By our lifestyle. The joy, love and righteousness of the Christian and the church is a powerful witness to the world around us and can be a strong introduction to Jesus (See John 13:34-35).

2. By sharing our faith. The apostle Peter urged the Christians to 'always be prepared to give an answer to everyone who asks you to give the reason for the hope you have' (1 Peter 3:15,16). In school, at work and on social occasions, people will ask questions and sometimes you will meet with opposition, but even this will give you opportunities to share the good news.

Have you had experience of this yet? ....

What happened? ....

....

Did you experience any difficulty? ....

3. By taking part in, praying for, and being involved with the evangelistic and missionary outreach of the church. As Timothy, Titus and others, and indeed whole churches, were swept up in Paul's missionary outreach, so by praying, giving or going, you can be involved in the spreading of the good news. Do you feel that you have a particular contribution to make in this?

....

BECOMING COMMITTED TO THE CHURCH

The Lord has given many lovely songs and hymns of praise to His church. Many of these speak of God's love to us or exhort us to love and worship Him, but also there are songs which speak of the love which we can experience within the family of God. One of these particularly sums up what we have been looking at in these last two lessons.

I thank You, Lord, that You don't want me
To make it on my own.
The day You showed me Your family
My spirit arrived at home.
Security I had never known.
Strength for my weakness is there.
My wealth, my rest and my liberty -
A living Jesus to share.
I thank You, Lord, that You don't want me
To make it on my own.
So I'll bless Your name and enjoy the love
My brothers and sisters have shown.

If you have repented of sin, believed on the Lord Jesus and know that you are a child of God, then you need to be part of the local church of the Lord Jesus. Having gone through the teaching in these lessons you should now have a good idea of what is involved in commitment to a local church. Seek the Lord in prayer about this: if you feel it is right for you to be part of the church, get in touch with your leaders. They may ask you to complete a form similar to the one overleaf.

Your pastor and elders will then also seek the mind of the Lord (or they and you may already know the will of God on this issue by now). If all feel it right, they will then receive you into the church on a suitable occasion, seeking to give you a real welcome in the name of the Lord and to commend you to God in prayer.

This course is yours to keep whether you join the church or not and you may find the notes useful for future reference.

SAMPLE FORM FOR SOMEONE WISHING TO JOIN THE CHURCH (The contents will be confidential to the leadership)

Name ....

Address ....

.... Phone ....

Immediate family ....

Age........................ Occupation..

Have you previously been a member of another church? ....

Have you left in good relationship? ....

When and where were you

Converted? ....

Baptised by immersion as a believer? ....

Baptised in the Spirit? ....

Do you have any particular skills which you would like to make available to the church? e.g. typing, carpentry, cooking, youth club experience, hospitality, gardening, music, etc.

....

....

If so, what level of skill have you reached and how free are you?

....

....

Would you like to know more about

Other church activities? ....

The covenant scheme for giving? ....

Is it your sincere desire to receive the ministry and teaching of the spiritual leaders of the church here and submit to their authority; to keep good relationships with other members of the church; to share, as you are able, in the upbuilding of the church; and to be committed to the regular gatherings of God's people?

Date: .... Signed: ....

For personal notes or questions you may want to ask your course leader.